GW00760300

Contents

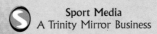

Sport Media
A Trinity Mirror Business

PRODUCED BY: Roy Gilfoyle & Jamie Dunmore **WRITTEN BY:** Paul Hassall
EXECUTIVE EDITOR: Ken Rogers **EDITOR:** Steve Hanrahan **ART EDITOR:** Rick Cooke **PRODUCTION EDITOR:** Paul Dove
WRITERS: David Randles, Chris McLoughlin, Gavin Kirk, John Hynes
DESIGN TEAM: Lee Ashun, Barry Parker, Colin Sumpter, Glen Hind, Alison Gilliland, James Kenyon

PHOTOGRAPHY: Trinity Mirror, Empics, John Cocks **PRINTERS:** Pensord
SALES & MARKETING MANAGER: Elizabeth Morgan 0151 285 8412
Write to: Sport Media, PO BOX 48, Liverpool, L69 3EB

FOWLER!

Let us pray

Fowler 1: 4-5

LIVERPOOL Football Club has been blessed with some of the greatest names ever to have played the beautiful game.

From the effervescent Emlyn Hughes and the cultured Alan Hansen through to the awesome Steven Gerrard and the King of them all, Kenny Dalglish, Anfield has developed into a haven for legends.

And yet when you wander through the illustrious names of players past and present, few have enjoyed the adulation that has been bestowed upon a certain Robbie Fowler.

He is arguably the most complete goalscorer the club has ever seen.

That in itself is some statement, given that over the years the club have had the likes of Gordon Hodgson, 'Sir' Roger Hunt, Kevin Keegan, Ian Rush and Michael Owen leading the line.

But ask anyone who has worked with the instinctive forward who is the most natural finisher to play for Liverpool and most – if not all – will point to Fowler.

Having attained legendary status while still in his teens, the Toxteth-born striker was quite possibly the finest frontman in the Premiership during the mid-90s and the memories of his goals will be forever etched in Liverpool folklore.

While the match at home to Charlton Athletic on May 13 marked Robbie's final appearance for the Reds in front of his adoring public at Anfield, it also gave fans the opportunity to thank the number nine for what he has done for Liverpool over the years.

It is with that in mind that we pay homage to the achievements of the man the fans simply call 'God'.

'The Toxteth-born striker was quite possibly the finest striker in the Premiership during the mid-90s'

FOWLER!

Saying goodbye to his followers

Robbie's Anfield farewell

Fowler 2: 6-9

'GOODBYE God.'

A simple message but one that meant so much to both player and fans alike.

After sharing so many wonderful memories down the years the standing ovation from all four corners of the ground was a fitting way for one of the finest Liverpool strikers of all time to bring his career at Anfield to a close.

All that was missing was a goal at the Kop end . . .

It had all seemed to be written in the script too, as Robbie, skipper for the day, took to the familiar turf one last time to rapturous applause against a side he had previously plundered eight goals in 10 appearances against.

But try as he might, the strike everyone was praying for did not arrive.

Half chances came and went as a lacklustre Reds team contrived to do their best to lose their final home match of the season.

His second spell at the club had not matched the heights of his first and with just minutes left came the twist of fate that summed up his last season as a Red.

Ahead of the clash with the relegated Londoners Rafa Benitez had made the decision to bring Robbie off before the final whistle in order to give him a priceless moment with his beloved supporters.

It was a touching sentiment but one that ultimately backfired for Robbie as the Reds were awarded a spot-kick at the Kop end less than two minutes after his emotional departure.

With Liverpool trailing 2-1, chants of "bring back Fowler" reverberated around the stadium as he watched ruefully from the bench.

FOWLER!

But it was not meant to be and Harry Kewell tucked away the penalty to secure third place and ensure Robbie's last match at Anfield did not end in defeat.

Speaking after the game the legendary number nine admitted that despite missing out on the chance to sign off in style, it had still been the farewell he had hoped for.

"I missed saying goodbye last time and I'm glad I could to do it this time," he said. "I'd have loved to have stayed but all good things come to an end. Thankfully I had a decent chance of saying goodbye. I've thanked the manager and the fans have been fantastic to me, in the first spell and probably just as good the second time around."

The game was almost a secondary event to what was billed as Robbie's big day and during an emotional lap of honour a visibly moved Fowler, flanked by his children, enjoyed what was to be his final moment on the hallowed turf.

"At the end, on the lap of honour when the fans were chanting my name, it was a bit of an emotional time but I did my best to keep the tears in," he said.

"With it being my last game at Anfield, I'd loved to have scored but not everything goes to plan in football. I tried not to get too carried away. I have had a good career at Liverpool and today I tried not to let things get on top of me and I think it worked. I felt I did alright."

As the final chapter on a glorious Anfield career came to a close, even Reds boss Rafa Benitez, the man who brought Robbie back to the club, was left ruing his decision to substitute the forward.

"I was just too quick," admitted Rafa.

"If I had waited a minute more, Robbie could have scored from the spot in front of the Kop – that would have been a perfect way to end for him. I wanted to give him the chance of a personal ovation, but it was just one of those things in the end. It was just bad luck for him, but at least I made sure he got the ovation he deserved."

FOWLER!

In the beginning . . .

ON April 9, 1975 Robert Bernard Fowler was born.

No-one would have thought it at the time, but he was destined to become a Kop legend.

From the age of six he longed to be a footballer and amidst the backdrop of the infamous Toxteth riots he set about achieving his dream, honing his raw ability in the local sports complex and the Davey Lewis Youth Club.

Looking back on his school days you may be surprised to hear that it wasn't 'God' or indeed Robbie Fowler who took the St Patrick's Primary School and the Nugent's Secondary School teams by storm.

Instead it was a shy, tiny youngster by the name of Robert Ryder who had the PE teachers purring.

Having taken his mother's maiden name, the nine-year-old excelled in St Patrick's Under-11s side and it wasn't long before he progressed into the Merseyside area team.

He started to catch the eye of watching scouts and after being rejected for England schoolboys, he made it into Bob Lynch's Liverpool Schoolboys side.

From here he went on to feature alongside Dele Adebola and future Everton midfielder Tony Grant in a team that won countless honours and it was during this successful period that he realised his ambition . . . to play and score at Goodison Park.

It is one of the most significant moments from his childhood as he fired home a double in a 5-0 Area Cup final win over Wirral Boys.

The goals continued to flow and his natural instinct for finding the back of the net convinced Reds scout Jim Aspinall he had found a potential star.

Persuading a boyhood Blue that his future was at Anfield was no mean feat but it was one Aspinall was determined to succeed in.

Speaking after the scout's death in 2004, Fowler expressed his appreciation for the man who had set him on the road to stardom.

"Jim was a lovely man," he said.

"He was the scout who spotted me and took me up to Liverpool. He spent a number of years there and he looked after me. I still kept in touch with him.

"We played Everton at Goodison in December last year and I got Jim tickets and he came and watched me. He died not long after."

Despite failing in his first attempt to lure the young hotshot to Anfield, Aspinall did not give up and for five years he tried to convince Robbie's dad that his son should sign for Liverpool.

Even the great Kenny Dalglish made efforts to sway the Fowler family.

But Bobby Fowler wanted Robbie to make the right choice and refused to commit his son's future to one club until they both felt the timing was right.

And so Robbie continued to train with Liverpool until finally the day came in 1991 when he decided they were the team for him. Aspinall wasted no time in whisking him up to Anfield and Robbie finally signed YTS forms with the Reds with the promise of a professional deal after three years.

Aspinall was overjoyed to get his man and by November 1994 Robbie had already proved his worth with a rise to prominence that saw him rewarded with a deal that confirmed his status as one of the hottest prospects in the game.

Man of the people: Robbie goes back to his roots for a kick about in Toxteth (far right) and became famous enough to have a play written about him called 'I Married Robbie Fowler'

Showing potential: Robbie (front, middle) in his schoolboy football days in the same team as Tony Grant and Dele Adebola – who both went on to become professional footballers in their own right

Baby faced: The pupils of St Patrick's Primary School got dressed up on their final day before moving up to secondary school. Robbie wore a nappy and drank from a bottle to play the part of a child as his friends (including Roy McParland, middle) were the parents. That doesn't explain the dodgy headgear though!

Picture supplied by James and Edna McParland

Making his mark (anti-clockwise from above): Fowler hits the target against Nottingham Forest and Chelsea, receives his first senior cap from Terry Venables and battles with Newcastle's Warren Barton

'Denis Law was positively purring at Fowler's natural way of taking chances'

When he could turn water into wine

The 1990s — Robbie at his best

WHEN Robbie Fowler hangs up his boots he could be forgiven for looking back on a glittering career with a hint of sadness.

Blessed with a mesmerising ability to score goals, he would have been a worthy addition to any of the trophy-laden sides that left their mark on Liverpool's glorious history.

But unfortunately for Robbie his era of brilliance came after the days of Shankly, Paisley, Fagan et al, and despite being the star man in Roy Evans' magnificent attacking side, they failed to claim the silverware they deserved.

Winners medals from two League Cups, one FA Cup and one UEFA Cup are by no means a meagre collection . . . but he could have won so much more.

The Premiership was in sight in 1996/97 but, unlike the sides of yesteryear, Roy Evans' men froze when it really mattered.

"I'm not sure we believed that we could win it, although we were top of the league for a number of weeks during the season," admitted Robbie in 2004.

"We just seemed to throw away silly points by losing games at home, like against Coventry. That was unheard of really. It was stupid little games like that where we should have been getting three points. When we saw the finishing line we just couldn't get across it."

Everyone is familiar with how Fowler burst onto the scene as a relatively unknown 18-year-old hitting 18 goals in 34 appearances in his first season.

It was some achievement for a rookie striker, but all the more impressive given that he missed seven weeks of the campaign as a result of a broken ankle suffered in an FA Cup clash with Bristol City.

It was the only low point of a wonderful debut season in which he struck his first Premier League goal

at home to Oldham Athletic to help the Reds rescue a 2-1 win from the jaws of defeat.

The five goals against Fulham and a hat-trick at home to Southampton will be the defining memories of his first campaign while a double in a 3-3 draw at Tottenham further enhanced his growing reputation, as did his first derby goal at Anfield.

The final home match of that season signalled the end of the standing Kop and although the Reds finished in a disappointing eighth place, Robbie's emergence gave fans hope for the future.

The 94/95 season marked Roy Evans' first full campaign in charge and it began in emphatic fashion as Liverpool thumped Crystal Palace 6-1 at Selhurst Park with Robbie wasting no time in getting off the mark.

A whirlwind hat-trick against Arsenal followed and anyone who may have questioned whether the young hotshot could recreate the form that had seen him make such a promising start to his career was soon put in their place.

The new-look Reds were playing

some stylish attacking football with Fowler the chief beneficiary as a double against Aston Villa in the league was swiftly followed by another brace in the 3-1 win at Ipswich Town.

Goals 15 and 16 for the season arrived in mid-November in a 3-1 win over Chelsea while he brought the New Year in with a bang with two more in a 4-0 romp at home to Norwich City on January 2.

He had already developed a habit for scoring vital goals and a solitary strike in each leg of the Coca-Cola Cup semi-final tie with Crystal Palace saw him fire the Reds to Wembley, where they defeated Bolton Wanderers 2-1.

It was a glorious occasion for the youngster and although he did not trouble the scoresheet, it was a special moment that saw him collect his first winners medal for Liverpool.

His sensational form earned him the PFA Young Player of the Year award and he completed a great week, in which he also celebrated his 20th birthday, by scoring a last minute winner at Arsenal. It was his 30th goal of the season.

The Reds rounded the campaign off on a high with a 2-1 win at home to Kenny Dalglish's champions, Blackburn Rovers,

with many tipping a youthful Reds side to make a strong challenge for the title in the 95/96 season.

The £8.5million arrival of Stan Collymore and a slack summer period saw Robbie dropped to the bench at the start of the season.

But with his first true challenge facing him, he responded in magnificent fashion, going on to form the most potent strike partnership in the league alongside 'Stan the Man.'

Highlights included four against Bolton in a 5-1 win at Anfield as well as a sublime double at Old Trafford as he upstaged Eric Cantona on his return from his Kung-Fu kick induced ban.

Another brace against United saw Roy Evans' men clinch a 2-0 home win while Arsenal were once again the victims of a Robbie hat-trick as they were gunned down 3-1 at Anfield.

Revelling alongside the mazy dribbles and inviting cut-backs of Steve McManaman and the power and crossing ability of Collymore, everything Robbie hit seemed to find the back of the net.

A wonder strike against Aston Villa where he bewildered Steve Staunton with a nutmeg before firing an unstoppable

rocket beyond Mark Bosnich helped the Reds to a 3-0 win over Aston Villa at Anfield and he would return to haunt Brian Little's side in the FA Cup semi-final just weeks later.

A bullet header gave the Reds the lead before an audacious volley that flew in off the upright booked another trip to Wembley.

The triumph set up a mouthwatering clash with Manchester United, but before he could contemplate another visit to the twin towers he was to play a huge role in the greatest Premiership match ever seen.

Both he and Collymore notched two apiece as the Reds came from behind to snatch a last-gasp 4-3 victory over title-chasing Newcastle United.

It was pure theatre and to this day provides a vivid but brutal reminder of why those two sides failed to break Manchester United's stranglehold on the title.

The attacking play was a joy to watch but from a defensive point of view there was certainly room for improvement.

Robbie's outstanding form in front of goal, not only saw him fire 36 goals in 53 matches, it also earned him another Young Player of the Year award. But despite grabbing another derby goal with a late

equaliser against Everton at Goodison Park, the season ended on a low note with an FA Cup final defeat against Manchester United . . . and a whole host of criticism for those white suits!

At this juncture few would have envisaged that the halcyon days of Robbie the 30-goals-a-season man were about to come to a premature end, but sadly that was the case as the 1996/97 season proved to be the last time he would reach the heights that saw him christened 'God.'

It was a slow start by his own high standards and by the beginning of October he had struck just two goals.

Stan Collymore's issues off the field had seen Patrik Berger replace him and support Robbie from an attacking midfield position, but although the prolific partnership was short of minutes on the pitch it wasn't long before the Reds' number nine was back on the goal trail.

Doubles against Derby and Swiss outfit FC Sion in the European Cup Winners Cup (ECWC) followed before he inevitably began to hit top form.

December brought with it an avalanche of six goals, including four against Middlesbrough, as the Reds surged towards the summit of the Premiership.

His second strike against Bryan Robson's side saw him notch up his 100th goal in just 165 matches – a total achieved one game ahead of his former strike partner and mentor, Ian Rush.

It was his first season in Europe too and he was determined to enjoy himself. A sensational strike against the Norwegians of Brann Bergen where he flicked the ball over the defence with his heel before racing through to volley past the keeper was yet another example of his genius.

With the Reds romping away at the top of the league Robbie hit a double in another 4-3 epic against Newcastle United, but it was a match that would prove their undoing and began a chain of defensive errors that would ultimately cost them the title.

His 30th of the season came in a 2-1 win at Sunderland but he would only score one further goal, against Paris St Germain in the ECWC semi-final defeat, before his campaign was cut short after he was sent off in a 1-1 derby draw at Everton.

The future was not as bright as we all would have hoped for and as injuries began to mount up, his dreams of winning the title with Liverpool looked destined to remain unfulfilled.

FOWLER!

Thou shalt not lie

Fowler 8: 22-23

FAMED for courting controversy both on and off the pitch, Robbie hit the headlines for all the right reasons (depending on your point of view!) in March 1997 when he sensationally tried to convince a referee not to give him a penalty.

The famous incident took place at Highbury, where Roy Evans' men were hoping to galvanise their title bid with a win over Arsene Wenger's Gunners.

Leading 1-0 in the second half the Reds looked set to double their advantage when Robbie appeared to be brought crashing to the ground by David Seaman.

Referee Gerald Ashby had no hesitation in pointing to the spot but as the Arsenal keeper appealed furiously, Robbie shocked the watching world when he began to shake his hand at the official in an attempt to change his mind.

Ashby later claimed not to have heard Fowler's appeals and stood by his decision.

It was probably not the brightest move to allow Robbie to take the kick, and although many fans believe he missed his kick on purpose, Jason McAteer was on hand to fire home the rebound.

The Reds went on to win the match 2-1 and Robbie received some well-deserved praise for his sporting conduct.

Arsenal boss Arsene Wenger was impressed by his actions but revealed his disappointment with Ashby.

"It is a great gesture by Fowler and I would like to give him an award for fair play," said Wenger. "But if he got that I would also have to give the referee an award for stupidity."

The Frenchman's words were echoed by Seaman, a friend of Fowler's from their time on England duty together.

"Our lads are still sick at the penalty decision but they all appreciate what Robbie tried to do," he said. "It just shows what a great man he is and I only wish the referee had also been big enough to admit a mistake."

PFA chief executive Gordon Taylor was also keen to express his view on the incident.

"People should be praising him for clearly admitting he didn't deserve a penalty and also for showing his concern that David Seaman, a fellow professional, might be sent off," he said.

"I know Robbie has a reputation for being a little bit of a scallywag on occasions, but nobody could fault him here. The pitch is always the best stage for players to show what they are made of."

The following day Robbie received another pat on the back, except this time it was from an even higher source, as he was handed a letter of thanks from the head of football's world governing body.

The fax from FIFA president Sepp Blatter hailed Robbie for his attempt to assist the referee and suggested he had acted for "the good of the game."

Having suffered at the hands of the Football Association and the media in the past, it was a nice change for Robbie, but one that lasted just over 24 hours, as the following day he received a £900 fine from UEFA for sporting a t-shirt backing the 500 Liverpool dockers who had been sacked, after scoring in a match with Norwegian outfit Brann Bergen at Anfield.

Hands up: Referee Gerald Ashby ignores the appeals of David Seaman (obscured) and Robbie Fowler and awards a penalty, which Jason McAteer (far left) scored from after Fowler's initial strike was saved
Left: What Sepp Blatter wrote to Fowler

'It shows what a great man he is and I only wish the referee had been big enough to admit his mistake'

Dear Robbie,

I want to congratulate you for the act of sportsmanship which you demonstrated last evening in the match between Liverpool and Arsenal. It is the kind of gesture which helps maintain the integrity of the game.

At a time when there is a disturbing trend towards cheating, and when FIFA is appealing to players (especially in the professional game) to help referees rather than deceive them, your example in this vital moment in such an important match should set an example to younger players and fellow professionals alike.

Thank you for helping FIFA in its efforts for the good of the game.

Yours sincerely,

FIFA
The General Secretary
J S Blatter

Saint and Sinner

WHETHER he's been goading opposition fans, invoking the wrath of the FA or simply showcasing his supreme talents in front of goal – it's fair to say Robbie Fowler has had an eventful career.

When the heavens above Anfield opened on that fateful night at home to Fulham back in 1993, God brought forth a flood of goals and with it came an endearing down-to-earth manner finely balanced by an impudence that created just as many headlines as match-winning performances.

From showing his buttocks to Leicester fans, offering support to the Liverpool dockers or questioning Graeme Le Saux's persuasion, he was never shy in expressing his point of view.

In fact you could probably compile an A-Z of Robbie's antics and only be scratching the surface.

Who could forget the moment he enraged Evertonians by snorting the white touchline in a 3-2 win over the Blues in 1999 or when he asked Frank De Boer "can we have our ball back, please?" during Barcelona's masterclass in possession football in our 3-1 Champions League defeat to the La Liga outfit in 2001.

Once again his tongue was firmly rooted in his cheek.

There are so many memories and all have been tinged with humour and controversy.

Suspensions, fines, headlines and goals – they all came hand in hand.

But it was this balance of imperfection and genius that endeared him to the Anfield faithful.

On netting a first minute effort at home to Middlesbrough in 1996 – a match in which he also grabbed his 100th goal for the Reds – he posed with Steve McManaman and quizzically glanced down at an imaginary watch. It was the type of cheeky celebration that we had come to expect from God.

Mention his name among Kopites and it will always raise a smile and an anecdote of a famous Robbie moment.

There were the times when you didn't know whether to laugh or groan as he went through the phase that saw him don bleached white hair and of course, who can forget the famous Fowler nose band?

The infamous Le Saux saga, culminating in FA disciplinary action. That's soon behind him though, as he shares a joke with Steven Gerrard (bottom)

But while his cheeky antics were often met with a cheer in the stands, they were frowned upon by football's authorities and at one point he regularly exited the FA headquarters with an empty wallet.

Gerard Houllier was also growing tired of Robbie's knack for courting trouble and following the controversy of an infamous training ground incident with Phil Thompson it seemed his mischievous nature would be one of the factors that would result in him leaving Liverpool.

When the day finally arrived he maintained his kinship with the Kop from afar and his four and five-finger salutes to bitter Manchester United fans showed he still had that cheeky Liverpudlian sense of humour that had made him such a darling among the followers in the stands.

A local lad, from a typically scouse background, he will be immortalised in Anfield folklore as one of the greatest strikers the club has seen.

Was he a spice boy or the controversial figure that the media liked to portray?

Not at all. To us he was quite simply . . . God.

Robbie responds to Everton fans after they question his
off-the-field activities and (right) lets cup success go to his head

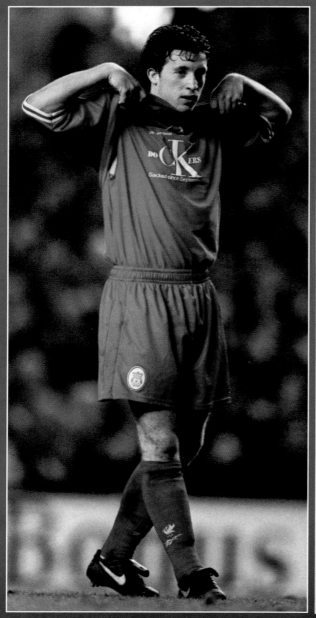

Robbie shows his
support for
Liverpool dockers
(left), while (right)
he finds it easier
than normal to put
this defender in
his pocket

Robbie celebrates a goal against
Newcastle (above) and amuses
Craig Bellamy in training (left)

Robbie shows concern
for a referee's eyesight

FOWLER!

A special relationship with God

Goals galore in the League Cup

FROM day one the League Cup would hold a special place in Robbie Fowler's heart.

It was the competition in which he made his goalscoring debut and proved to be the one in which he became an overnight star.

His six-goal salvo over two legs against Fulham in 1993 set him on the road to becoming one of the most lethal strikers in Premiership history and from that moment on he would have a happy knack of scoring in English football's second cup competition - ending with 29 goals in total.

The 1994/95 season saw him hit two goals in two matches against Burnley in round two as the Reds began their march towards Wembley.

In a tight semi-final with Crystal Palace he popped up in injury-time to fire home Steve McManaman's low cross to net his 24th goal of the season and give the Reds a vital first leg advantage to take to Selhurst Park.

And he repeated the trick in the second leg in London when his clever run kept him onside, allowing him to advance on to McManaman's through ball and slide the ball into the net after drawing out Nigel Martyn.

It gave the Reds a comfortable 2-0 aggregate victory and set them up for the final with Bruce Rioch's Bolton

Wanderers, which they won 2-1.

The goals started to flow again a year later and an audacious lob secured the Reds' progress past Sunderland in round two.

Manchester City were the victims in round three at Anfield with Robbie netting one of four without reply as the Reds cantered to victory.

But a miserable run in November began with the Reds crashing out of the competition courtesy of a 1-0 defeat at home to Newcastle United – thus ending their hopes of retaining the trophy.

By now Fowler had established himself as one of the finest strikers in Europe and, although he was regularly setting the world alight in the Premiership, he still enjoyed a special relationship with the League Cup.

The 1996/97 season began with the Reds hoping to sustain a serious title challenge but Robbie had started more slowly this time.

However, it was in the League Cup that he boosted his confidence and after scoring the goal that earned the Reds a replay at Charlton, he hit a double at Anfield to ensure Liverpool progressed with a 4-1 win.

Arsenal were waiting in round four and Robbie proved to be a thorn in their side once more as he fired a brace in a 4-2 win.

But unfortunately there was to be no League Cup glory on this occasion as Middlesbrough put paid to our hopes in the next round.

A goal against West Brom a year on saw the Reds through a tricky away tie but they were unceremoniously dumped out of the competition weeks later as Tottenham ran riot at Anfield in a 3-1 win that proved to be the last straw for Roy Evans in his joint managerial position with Gerard Houllier.

An extra-time goal against Newcastle in the 1997/98 season helped the Reds to a 2-0 win and gave them the momentum that took them into a semi-final clash with Middlesbrough.

But despite giving Liverpool a slender first leg advantage with a late strike in a 2-1 win at Anfield, medal number two would elude Robbie for the time being as the Reds crashed out at the Riverside.

By the following year injury had begun to take its toll but he still managed his obligatory League Cup goal when he dispatched a penalty in a 3-1 win over Kevin Keegan's Fulham in round three.

His knee injury had robbed him of the mobility that had seen him become one of the great goalscorers of his generation but, although he was no longer a definite starter in the Reds' first team, he emerged as the main man in the League Cup success of 2001.

Having struggled to find the net in the opening months of the season he got the ball rolling with the relief of an extra-time winner against Chelsea in round three.

A hat-trick followed in round four as he inspired Liverpool to their biggest ever away victory in the League Cup – 8-0 at Stoke City.

A last-minute effort against Crystal

FOWLER!

Palace in the semi-final second leg put the seal on an emphatic 5-0 win before he took centre stage in the final when he picked up his second winners medal and was man of the match as he scored and helped the Reds beat Birmingham City on penalties.

A five season sabbatical followed before he was back scoring League Cup goals for Liverpool, with an exquisite opening goal in the 4-3 win over Reading.

It meant he became the second highest League Cup goalscorer in Liverpool's history and capped a night that saw him captain the Reds for the first time since 2001.

But for all his achievements for the Reds while on League Cup duty, his final goal in the competition came in one of Liverpool's most embarrassing defeats of recent times as they were hammered 6-3 at Anfield by Arsenal in round five in early 2007.

Robbie hits a hat-trick (above) against Stoke in the glorious 2000/01 campaign and he is at it again (right), scoring against Chelsea

Turning the other cheek

Houllier on Fowler, Fowler on Houllier

IT IS fair to say that Gerard Houllier and Robbie Fowler did not always see eye to eye.

The Frenchman was one for discipline and order, while Robbie was . . . well, he was just Robbie.

No-one could doubt that Houllier was a big fan of Fowler's ability, but he could never quite come to terms with a character who was shadowed by controversy and who had been an integral member of the Roy Evans era.

Robbie admits that he still harbours some resentment towards his former boss at the way he felt he was forced out of the club he loves, but it is also important to remember that while he did not enjoy the Frenchman's iron rule, it was under Houllier that he had his most successful period of his career in terms of silverware.

Houllier:

"I think Robbie made a mistake in wanting to leave. He should have been more patient.

"He had to work more on his fitness on the back of several operations and when you see the progress other players have made then I would say it was a mistake to go.

"In modern football players don't play 60 games a season, only the managers do and that's why we are so tired!

"I understand with his status with the fans and his achievements why it was right to move on when he did.

"Letting someone you like and who the fans like leave is always a difficult decision to make but that's a manager's job. I don't think we had a choice because he wanted to go."

Feeling regretful about Fowler's move to Leeds

"That was the best Robbie has played for a long time, and I'm delighted to say he's gradually getting back to his best. I'm pleased with the way he's playing and the way he has overcome his problems. You feel for all your players, you like all your players and when they have problems and difficulties you try hard to be supportive."

Saluting another Fowler comeback after the striker notched a double in a 3-0 win over West Ham in February 2001

"I think Robbie is taking some unfair criticism. He's just gone to the club, it's his third club in three years and he needs to settle. We know his quality."

Standing up in defence of Fowler following a difficult start to his Manchester City career in December 2003

"We won't keep anyone here who is unhappy. Robbie knows that he has been part of my plans and he knows all that I have done for him this season. But if he is not happy with that, he can leave. All he has to do is come and see me and I won't stand in his way."

It seems the writing is on the wall in June 1999

"Robbie is one of the top strikers in Europe and I was very concerned by what I was repeatedly reading about him leaving the club. I'm delighted that he's staying because he will play a huge part in the plans we are now putting in place for the future here."

But it all seems rosy again following clear-the-air talks just weeks later

"Robbie has been working extremely well and has waited for his chance. It will come and he's part of my plans. He is a high-profile player, but I have three England strikers and I can only play two most of the time."

Defending his decision not to pick Fowler more regularly, September 2001

Robbie:

"The result was secondary because we were all worried about Gerard's health. He underwent a big operation, as everyone knows, but he seems to be doing really well and it will be good to see him back in harness when he gets the go-ahead."

"David O'Leary and Gerard are big pals. Our gaffer speaks to him regularly and I'm told Gerard still asks about me, which is nice. Gerard's record has been phenomenal over the last couple of years since he took charge and the players owe a lot to him."

Concern for Houllier in his attempts to regain his health in 2002

"I got on well with them all. Obviously myself and Gerard Houllier had differences of opinion but there were times when we did get on as well."

Admitting he enjoyed some good times with Houllier as well as bad ones

"I obviously believed that I should have been playing and he obviously believed that he had a better pairing up front. I didn't necessarily agree with him but he was the manager and you have to live by his decisions.

"I was always led to believe that a captain should be playing. I didn't go in and say that but I just went in one game and said: 'Listen, it's pointless me being vice-captain and not playing'. Gerard Houllier took off at me."

Revealing his strained relationship with Houllier in his autobiography

FOWLER!

The holy trinity of a cup treble

Fowler 12: 34-37

FOLLOWING a catalogue of injuries and off-the-field problems, Fowler went into the 2000/01 season determined to recapture the form that had made him one of the most feared strikers in the Premiership.

However, the arrival of Emile Heskey at the end of the 1999/2000 campaign had put his first team place in jeopardy, and with the Reds fighting for honours on four fronts Gerard Houllier was determined to make full use of his squad.

This meant Robbie was in the side one week, but out of it the next. It was frustrating for a man who had once been the first name on the team sheet.

But they say that the cream always rises to the top and despite a series of appearances as a substitute, he came good when it mattered most to play a key role in our march towards treble glory.

Here are some of Robbie's best moments in that treble season . . .

1 League Cup third round, November 1, 2000
Liverpool 2
Chelsea 1 *aet*
Fowler struck the winner in extra-time when he squeezed Patrik Berger's incisive pass into the bottom right hand corner to set us on the road to Cardiff at the expense of Chelsea.

2 League Cup fourth round, November 29, 2000
Stoke City 0
Liverpool 8
Despite having scored just one goal

in the Premiership since the start of the season, Robbie continued his prolific strike rate in the League Cup by notching his ninth hat-trick for Liverpool as the Reds ran riot at the Britannia Stadium.

3 Premiership, December 23, 2000
Liverpool 4
Arsenal 0
On as a late substitute for Michael Owen, God got himself in on the action when he latched on to a through ball and swept the ball past the advancing Alex Manninger.

It was yet another goal against the Gunners and reiterated Liverpool's status as a growing force under Gerard Houllier.

4 League Cup, semi-final, 2nd leg, January 24, 2001
Liverpool 5
Crystal Palace 0
Robbie's League Cup love affair continued with a last minute strike that put the seal on an emphatic victory and booked our first trip to Anfield South that season.

'After being omitted from the starting line-up, he replaced Heskey and made an immediate impact'

FOWLER!

5 Premiership,
February 3, 2001
Liverpool 3
West Ham United 0
A goal from God either side of half-time helped the Reds on their way to a comfortable 3-0 win and kept Houllier's men in with a shout of Champions League football next season.

6 League Cup final,
February 25, 2001
Liverpool 1
Birmingham City 1 *aet*
Liverpool won 5-4 on penalties
Named as skipper for the day, Robbie gave Liverpool control of the match with a stunning volley from 25 yards out.

It was not enough to secure victory though and when the match went to a penalty shoot-out he was on hand to coolly slot home the Reds' penultimate kick – the perfect way to cap a man of the match display.

7 FA Cup sixth round,
March 11, 2001
Tranmere Rovers 2
Liverpool 4
An entertaining Merseyside derby went the way of the Reds as Fowler fired home a late spot-kick to rule out any fears of an upset.

8 Premiership,
March 31, 2001
Liverpool 2
Manchester United 0
A stunning first half display saw Liverpool put the champions-elect to the sword at Anfield.

After Steven Gerrard had given the Reds the lead after 15 minutes, Robbie doubled the advantage when he took down the midfielder's exquisite pass and smashed a magnificent volley beyond Barthez.

9 FA Cup semi-final,
April 8, 2001
Liverpool 2
Wycombe Wanderers 1
A sublime free-kick seven minutes from time doubled the Reds' advantage and was enough to secure yet another trip to the Millennium Stadium – this time for the FA Cup final.

10 Premiership,
April 22, 2001
Liverpool 3
Tottenham 1
On as a 39th minute substitute for the injured Emile Heskey, Robbie had to wait until two minutes from time to seal victory when he headed home Markus Babbel's accurate right-wing cross.

11 UEFA Cup final,
May 16, 2001
Liverpool 5
Alaves 4 *aet*
Liverpool won with a golden goal
A rollercoaster final between two so-called defensive sides looked to have been won by Robbie's late solo effort.

Despite having to endure the disappointment of being omitted from the starting XI, he replaced Emile Heskey just after the hour mark and made an immediate impact.

On 73 minutes he burst into the area and held off three challenges

before drilling a right foot strike into the far corner to give the Reds a 4-3 lead.

However, it was not the end of the scoring and a last minute goal from Jordi took the match into extra-time and robbed God of the chance to be the match winner.

12 Premiership,
May 19, 2001
Charlton 0
Liverpool 4
Needing a final day victory at Charlton, the Reds produced a scintillating second half performance to secure Champions League football for the following season.

After struggling in the first period, Fowler settled the nerves on 55 minutes with a magnificent overhead effort that flew into the top corner.

Liverpool took control from then on and after Danny Murphy had doubled the lead, Robbie rifled in a great effort 19 minutes from time to ensure the remainder of the match was a formality.

Robbie wheels away (top) after scoring against Birmingham in the League Cup final, and lifts the FA Cup (bottom) after a thrilling final against Arsenal

Performing miracles

GOD'S TOP 5 GOALS

HE is capable of the sublime and the audacious, and like all great strikers he has the knack for scoring vital goals.

But when you've got 183 to choose from just how do you go about choosing Robbie Fowler's top five Liverpool goals?

It's not an easy task. Even the great man himself admits to having trouble picking a definitive list. But then such is the calibre of his finishing that any number of efforts could be chosen as one of his best.

With this in mind we felt there was no better way to pick a top five than to ask the people who know all about his finishing . . . the fans.

The subject created much interest and debate and there were more than one or two disagreements, but after enlisting the help of fans website thisisanfield.com we finally managed to come to a decision and we can now reveal what we believe to be God's holy quintnet.

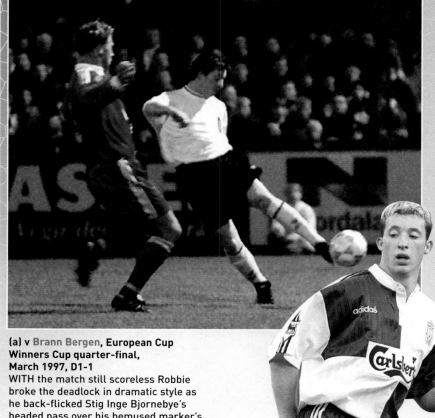

(a) v Brann Bergen, European Cup Winners Cup quarter-final, March 1997, D1-1
WITH the match still scoreless Robbie broke the deadlock in dramatic style as he back-flicked Stig Inge Bjornebye's headed pass over his bemused marker's head before racing into the penalty area and unleashing a devastating volley beyond the keeper.

(a) v Manchester United, Premiership, October 1995, D2-2
AFTER receiving Jamie Redknapp's pass in the inside left channel he drove into the box and unleashed a venomous drive into the near post top corner to leave Peter Schmeichel with no chance.

(n) v Birmingham City, **Worthington Cup final, February 2001, D1-1, won 5-4 on pens**
PLAYING in his first final in five years Robbie got the Reds off to the perfect start when he ran onto Emile Heskey's flick-on and with his first touch volleyed an unstoppable 25-yard effort over the despairing dive of the keeper.

(h) v Aston Villa, **Premiership, March 1996, W3-0**
STEVE McManaman played the ball into Fowler and in one swift movement he flicked the ball through Steve Staunton's legs and ran in on goal before unleashing a quite stunning 25-yard drive into the far corner.

(n) v Aston Villa, **FA Cup semi-final, March 1996, W3-0**
SHOWING superb awareness, Fowler anticipated that Jamie Redknapp's left-wing free-kick would be cleared and dropped to the edge of the penalty area.
As the ball fell his way he chested the ball down and executed a sublime volley that flew in off the upright to virtually book a place at Wembley.

FOWLER!

Leaving the promised land

When Robbie had to seek pastures new

AFTER scoring 171 goals in 330 games and establishing himself as one of the most lethal marksmen to have ever worn a red shirt, November 30, 2001, was to mark a sad day in the eventful life of Robbie Fowler.

In 15 years with Liverpool Football Club he had endured the full range of emotions and yet finally the unthinkable had become a reality – he was leaving.

For Robbie and fans alike, it was the end of an era.

From an 11-year-old hopeful to the star man of a side that failed to secure the Premiership title their talent deserved, he evolved into a frustrated substitute in Gerard Houllier's heroic treble winning team.

The mid-90s had been full of personal glory and yet the memories of a sprightly 18-year-old firing home goals for fun had been juxtaposed with the images of an injury-jinxed number nine who could no longer command a regular starting place.

His departure had been on the cards for several months but, although he had been mentally preparing himself for the moment he would have to say a sad farewell to his friends at Melwood, it was still a day of mixed emotions when he finally completed an £11million move to Leeds United.

On announcing his decision to join the Elland Road club he spoke glowingly about the potential of David O'Leary's side but, as he revealed years later, he knew deep

down that it was not the right decision.

Speaking as a Manchester City player in 2003, he revealed his anguish at having to leave the club he grew up at.

"I was gutted to leave in the first place," he said.

"I'd been at Liverpool since I was 11 and when the time came to go it was upsetting. I felt like crying because a big part of me had been taken away. I wanted to go so that I could play first team football but deep down I didn't want to leave and it was a massive wrench."

The nature of Robbie's departure meant that he never had the opportunity to say a proper farewell to the fans and he was particularly disappointed that his last game at Anfield ended with him being substituted when Dietmar Hamann was sent off against Sunderland on November 25, 2001.

He explained: "If I could change anything it would be my last game for Liverpool.

"I got brought off at half-time against Sunderland and we were winning 1-0. We had a man sent off and for me there are no words to describe it.

"I more or less knew I would be leaving and it was horrible not being able to say goodbye to the fans. If there was one thing I could change it would be that more than anything else. It was even worse than losing the FA Cup to Man U, being left out of the starting line-up for cup finals and the cream suits!"

'The thing I'll miss most about Anfield is the fans. They were always top quality'

Reaction

"The prospect of Fowler playing for us excites me. Over time, if we can train him and fit him into our way of playing, then he is somebody who can score a lot of goals for us."
DAVID O'LEARY, Leeds United manager

"It wasn't our decision to let him go. Robbie wanted to go and to see a local boy moving on is a sad thing for the club. More than most he found it difficult to fit in with the rotation system. I can understand that he found it hard. Robbie felt that a move at this moment in time would help his career and you have to respect that. He felt the time was right to move on and it was his decision."
PHIL THOMPSON, Liverpool caretaker boss

"There's no doubt that the thing I will miss most about Anfield will be the fans. They were always top quality and gave me tremendous support through the good and bad times. Thanks to everyone for your support.

"Once the move has gone through, I'll have new supporters and I know all about how fantastic the Leeds faithful are. I'll admit, it will feel slightly odd pulling on the white shirt for the first time but I'm a professional footballer, so it won't be a problem at all."
ROBBIE FOWLER

"Robbie called me on Tuesday and told me the two clubs had agreed a fee and that he would be going. He was a bit upset when I spoke to him and I know for a fact that it's breaking his heart to leave, but he feels he needs first team football and that's understandable.

"It took me by surprise but I guess this is something Robbie feels he has to do. I wish him all the best."
JAMIE REDKNAPP

"Unfortunately, there is a time for some players to leave a football club and I think that time for Robbie and Liverpool is now.

"He's hardly played any games, his contract is up in 19 months and Liverpool can't afford to run the risk of losing out completely as they did with Steve McManaman."
MARK LAWRENSON

"I can understand the fans' concern. Leeds now look serious contenders. But whatever people may fear, Phil Thompson and Gerard Houllier would not have sold Robbie if they did not think they could cope. They have won five trophies in the past year, so they know what they are doing.

"Ideally, they'd have sold Robbie abroad, but Leeds had the money. It just wasn't working out for Robbie or Liverpool. His body language wasn't right and he needed a fresh start.

"The time was right to sell him."
JOHN ALDRIDGE

"There was a very real prospect of us signing him, but his first choice was Leeds, although we were a close second.

"I have known Robbie Fowler since he was a boy and I have always felt that he is the best finisher in the British game. I believe he will prove that now at Leeds."
GRAEME SOUNESS, Blackburn Rovers boss

"The departure of Fowler saddens me, but does not surprise me."
KENNY DALGLISH

'There aren't many strikers like Robbie around these days, not just in England but in Europe. In his prime he was one of the best finishers there's ever been.'

Steven Gerrard

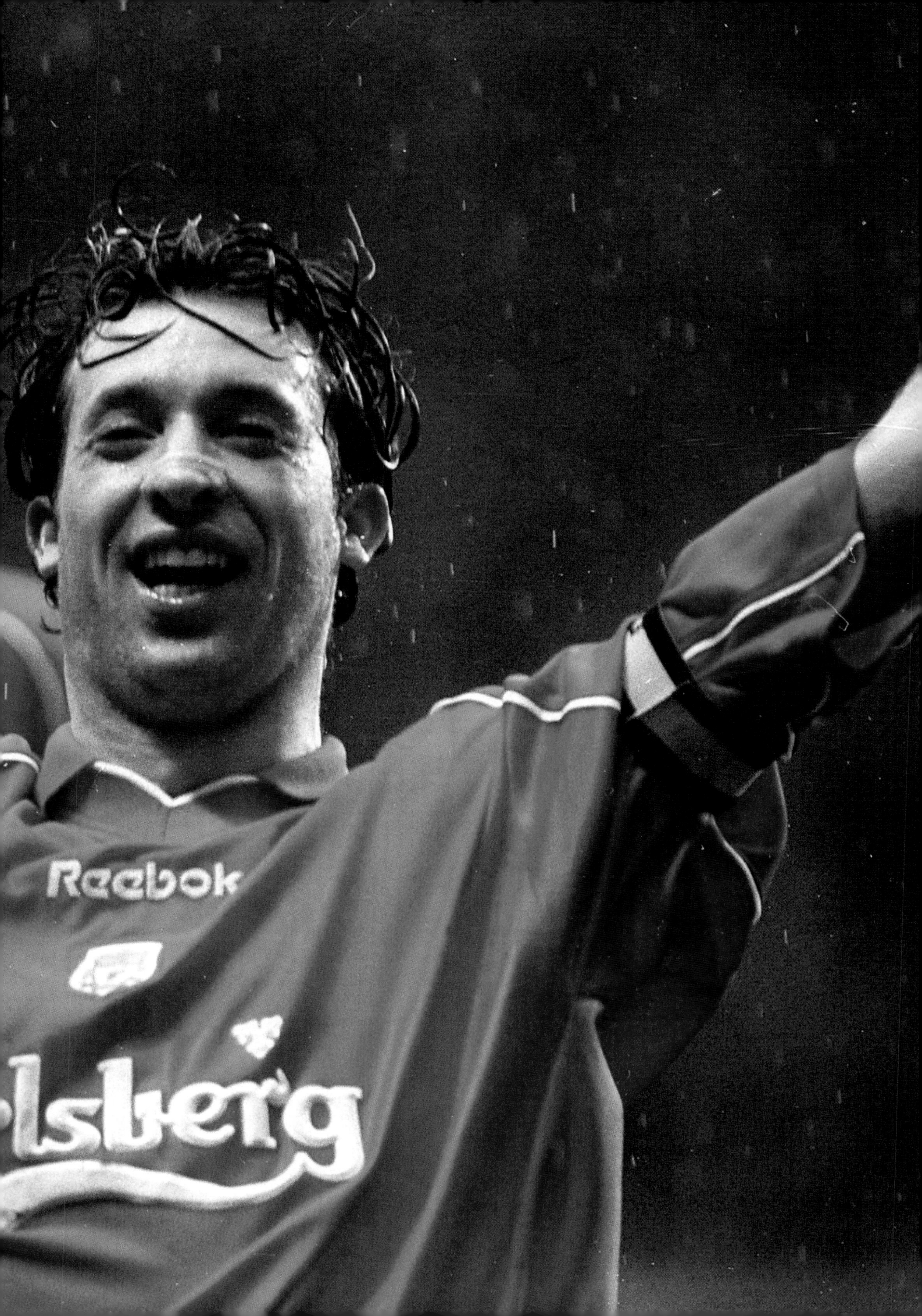
Reebok

'Just as people were writing him off, he produced the form that earned a move back to Anfield'

CAREER AWAY FROM LIVERPOOL			
	Spell	Games	Goals
Leeds United	2001-3	33	14
Man City	2003-6	80	21

The time spent in the wilderness

IT was one of those strange coincidences that seems unique to football that saw Robbie Fowler's Leeds United debut take place at the same venue where his career had begun.

As he ran out at Craven Cottage in the unfamiliar yellow away strip of his new side his mind must have wandered back to that moment eight years earlier when he had made his Reds bow.

On that occasion he had announced himself to the football world with a superb debut strike and he was keen to repeat the trick for Leeds United.

Linking up with Harry Kewell and Mark Viduka he showed some neat touches and, although there was to be no goal against Fulham this time around, the early promise soon bore fruit against Everton when he scored a brace in a 3-2 win.

David O'Leary had given him the run of games he needed to recapture his match sharpness and Robbie had begun to repay him with goals – 12 in 23 appearances, including a hat-trick in a 3-0 win at Bolton.

But all was not rosy in the Leeds United garden and, despite leading the Premiership at the turn of the year, they suffered a second half of the season collapse that saw them finish in fifth place.

There were problems off the field too and after the revelations of a huge debt, they sacked David O'Leary in the summer and began to sell off their prized assets.

It had been a disastrous spell for Robbie personally, as a pre-season hip injury ruled him out of the first few months of the 02/03 campaign.

By now Terry Venables had been drafted in to try and save a sinking ship but Robbie made just two more starts before being offloaded to Manchester City in January.

At City he only managed two goals in the remainder of that season.

Not even an injury-time equaliser in a 2-2 draw at home to Liverpool in November 2003 could kick-start his career.

When things failed to improve during the rest of that campaign he contemplated retirement.

But both Kevin Keegan and Stuart Pearce convinced him that he still had a role to play and in the second half of the 04/05 season he fired his 150th Premiership goal in City's 3-2 win at home to Norwich.

He looked to be ending the season on a high but when he failed to score a late penalty in the final match of the season against Middlesbrough, it denied the Eastlands side a place in the UEFA Cup.

Fuelled by a desire to make amends for his miss Robbie was hopeful of making a fresh start in the 2005/06 season, but once again injury would thwart his efforts.

It all seemed like a case of 'same old story' but just as people were beginning to write him off, he produced the form that ultimately earned him his move back to Anfield.

A rare start saw him strike a hat-trick against Scunthorpe in the FA Cup before he memorably taunted the Manchester United fans with a five-fingered salute after scoring the third in a 3-1 derby win.

It was a trick he was keen on, having previously riled the United fans by holding up four fingers in the pre-Istanbul days.

It may not be the fondest memory City fans have of Fowler, but it is certainly the image all Reds will remember vividly when they think of Robbie in a blue shirt.

Fowler 16: 46-49

Spreading the word

England calls for Fowler effect

A GOALSCORING phenomenon at club level, Robbie Fowler proved to be something of an enigma on the international scene.

Blessed with an innate ability to score goals, a combination of injuries, Alan Shearer and sheer bad luck over the years prevented 'God' from establishing himself at the forefront of England's attack.

Indeed, for a man of his talent, an international career of just 26 caps is a somewhat meagre reward considering his prolific strike rate for Liverpool during the 1990s.

The fact that 15 of those appearances came as a substitute tells the story of a footballer who was rarely given the opportunity to showcase his ability on the world stage.

And yet, at first, he had seemed destined to follow in the footsteps of some of the greatest forwards to have ever play for England.

After making his debut as a 76th minute substitute during the 1-0 friendly win over Bulgaria in March 1996, he made his first start for his country the following month in a 0-0 draw at home to Croatia.

It was hardly the most inspiring game to lay down a marker for the future but it was enough to convince Terry Venables that he was worthy of a place in his squad for Euro '96.

Venables said of Fowler: "There is definitely a bit of the Jimmy Greaves instinct in him.

"Jim used to pass the ball into the net, though he did hit some rockets. Robbie can do the same."

However, the partnership of Alan Shearer and Teddy Sheringham meant the 21-year-old hotshot was forced to settle for a place on the bench throughout the tournament and he was restricted to a bit-part role as a substitute in the 4-1 win over Holland and the quarter-final penalty shoot-out victory over Spain.

Despite failing to find the net in his first five outings it was inevitable that Fowler would score for his country and under the new regime of Glenn Hoddle he fired two in two matches in friendly victories over Mexico and Cameroon.

But still he could not convince the England hierarchy that he was worthy of a regular place in the side, and when serious injury struck in February 1998 he was cruelly ruled out of the World Cup in France.

It was a twist of fate that would see his club team-mate Michael Owen fire his way towards global stardom and further reduce Fowler's chances of securing a long-term future as England's number nine.

Persistent injuries not only threatened his place in the England squad but also led to what had seemed unthinkable as he lost his ❯

place in the Reds' first XI to Emile Heskey.

He finally put two seasons of injury frustration behind him when he fired home the opener in a 2-0 win over the Ukraine in May 2000 – almost three years after his last international goal.

But it was not enough for Robbie to force his way into the side for the ill-fated Euro 2000 campaign under Kevin Keegan.

The arrival of Sven Goran Eriksson as manager offered him a brief resurgence and he added to his England tally with goals against Mexico and Albania.

His last start came in the 2-2 draw with Greece in October 2001, a match that saw England book their place in the World Cup Finals in Japan/South Korea.

Despite finally making his World Cup debut at the age of 27, his one and only appearance as a substitute – in the 3-0 second round win over Denmark – would also prove to be God's last game for his country.

ENGLAND UNDER-18s

A YOUTHFUL Fowler was part of a talented Under-18 squad which captured the country's imagination when they stormed to glory in the European Championships in England.

Robbie emerged as the star of the tournament as he top scored with an impressive five goals.

The highlight of the competition was his hat-trick against Spain in a decisive 5-1 win during the group phase.

ENGLAND UNDER-21s

ROBBIE continued on from his scoring debut for Liverpool with a strike after just three minutes of his Under-21 bow in a 4-0 win away to San Marino on November 17, 1993.

But despite his fine start, he was always destined for the senior squad and played just eight games for the Under-21s, scoring three goals.

THE GOALS

1 England 2 (Sheringham 19, Fowler 55) **Mexico 0**
Friendly, Wembley, March 29, 1997

2 England 2 (Scholes 44, Fowler 45) **Cameroon 0**
Friendly, Wembley, November 15, 1997

3 England 2 (Fowler 44, Adams 68) **Ukraine 0**
Friendly, Wembley, May 31, 2000

4 England 4 (Fowler 14, Beckham 29, Scholes 35, Sheringham 74) **Mexico 0**
Friendly, Pride Park, May 25, 2001

5 England 2 (Owen 43, Fowler 87) **Albania 0**
World Cup qualifier, St James' Park, September 5, 2001

6 England 1 (Fowler 63) **Italy 2** (Montella 67, 90 (pen))
Friendly, Elland Road, March 27, 2002

7 Cameroon 2 (Eto'o 5, Geremi 58) **England 2** (Vassell 12, Fowler 90)
Friendly, Universiade Memorial, Kobe, Japan, May 26, 2002

ENGLAND STATS

PLAYED	W	D	L	GOALS
26	15	8	3	7

FOWLER!

The prodigal son returns

God's Prayer

Fowler 17: 50-53

Our Fowler, thou art is scoring,
Robbie be thy name,
To Anfield come,
Thy transfer has been done,
On a free as it is in January,
Give us this day our favourite Red,
And Alonso will give you the best passes,
As Carra stops those who pass against us,
Deliver us the title,
And lead us not into relegation,
For nine is your number forever and ever,
Our man.

FIRST GOAL BACK

THERE was more than a slight case of déjà vu when Robbie Fowler struck his first goal since returning to Liverpool.

Okay, it took him a little longer than during his first spell at the club when he scored on his debut but, just as in September 1993, the victims were once again Fulham.

It was his ninth game back and proved to be a case of fourth time lucky after he had had three efforts ruled out prior to the match against the Cottagers.

Starting alongside Fernando Morientes in attack it was his 16th minute effort that broke the deadlock when he nodded home a poacher's goal at the far post.

It was a poignant moment for our new number 11 as it put him level with Kenny Dalglish in fifth place in the club's all-time scoring list with 172 goals for Liverpool.

Having come under criticism for their lack of cutting edge prior to the match Robbie's effort inspired the Reds to go on a goal spree, hitting five past Chris Coleman's shell-shocked side.

Delighted scorer Fowler said after the game: "It's been a long time coming.

"It doesn't matter that it wasn't at the Kop end. A goal is a goal no matter which end it goes in."

Praising God from on high

WHEN Rafa Benitez made the shock swoop to bring Robbie Fowler back to Anfield it was a move that bordered on genius.

If the legendary striker could contribute a few goals and help the Reds turn their possession into wins it would be a gamble well worth taking – and if he didn't, then it had cost the club next to nothing.

For Robbie it was the realisation of a dream he had thought would never materialise and a chance he will always be grateful to Rafa for.

His final season at the club may not have seen him play as many games as he would have liked, but with his initial impact he repaid Rafa's faith with a number of important goals and his influence off the pitch proved to be just as important as his contributions on it.

Rafa:

"I can't wait to see him scoring his first goal again in front of the Kop but we must work with him to improve his physical condition.

"People have told me all about him and what he can do for the team. He has good memories here and hopefully there will be a lot more in the future.

"First of all he's a good finisher and secondly he gives us more alternatives. We can use Cisse on the right and still always have another player near the box.

"I knew the player. We remember the UEFA Cup final against Alaves and we knew what he could do.

"He gets more than 10 goals every season, sometimes a lot more. He's a good finisher."
Revealing his expectations of Robbie in January 2006

"It's good for the competitiveness to have Robbie here.

"If the players don't understand that they have to work hard, always, at this level, then they should not be playing. Robbie's arrival will help things.

"If you have more players competing for the same position that makes everyone work harder. We're creating chances but we do need to score more goals.

"Now, with Robbie, we have more competition up front. When we decided to sign him, we knew we were signing a player who needs to work hard. I've told him that. He's a player who can score a lot of goals and give other players things we need."
Explaining the benefits of competition for places

"I think for some of the younger players Robbie is an idol.

"And to see your idol in front of you and see the things he can do is amazing for some of them.

"He is really good and really positive, a very good signing and he now has the mentality that you look for in a senior player of his age.

"He trains at the same level as the rest of the other players in every training session. If you see the number of goals that he scores in training it's fantastic. You see that in every training session."
Hailing Robbie the idol, October 2006

"We know Robbie's record is amazing in this competition.

"But if we play like this and create lots of chances then he can score goals in all competitions. He has the quality.

"Robbie played well because he has game intelligence and quality, and he is a very good finisher as he showed by his fantastic goal.

"It was a very good finish. I have seen him in training every day and he is very good. Only people with his quality can do this."
After Robbie took second place in the all-time list of Liverpool goalscorers in the League Cup with a strike against Reading in October 2006

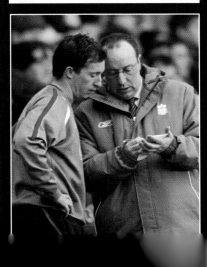

"The thing about Robbie is, he doesn't play for money as he plays for the love of this club. That is very difficult and rare to find these days in football.

"With a pre-season, he [Fowler] will be fitter, and he has the game intelligence. He always scores goals and can give us a lot of things. He plays with passion."
Praising Robbie's passion after offering him a one-year contract in the summer of 2006

"If Robbie is fit, he could play for any club in the world. He's such a good player. He's been knocking the goals in during training already. It's clear that when it comes to scoring goals he's a natural. If you haven't got £100m to spend every year and want to get to the top, you must use your imagination. We've done that with Robbie."
On using his imagination to sign Robbie, January 2006

Robbie:

"The manager has spent well. This squad is a much better squad and any player coming in will be very impressed looking around the dressing room. What they achieved last year (winning the Champions League) was fantastic. If I can help in any way then it is beneficial to me and the club."
Praising his new boss, January 2006

"I haven't played under him before but results within the past year have been fantastic. I've heard nothing but good reports from everyone involved in the club - from players to supporters. It's something I am excited about."
On the prospect of playing under Benitez, January 2006

"You can imagine how happy I was when the manager offered me another year. This is something I have wanted for a long time.

"When I signed, the manager told me he would look at the situation at the end of the season. He's had a look at what I've done and thankfully I've been given the best possible answer.

"I feel as though I've done alright and the manager has been pleased with me as well. I'm looking forward to next season now."
Showing his delight at being

WARNING
GOALKEEPING HAZARD

HAT-TRICKS

It's as easy as one, two, three . . . and sometimes four or five!

FOWLER
9

Fowler 20: 58-61

IN his prime Robbie Fowler was the archetypal hat-trick man.

It was a habit that had come naturally since his early years with Liverpool Schoolboys and one he continued when he burst onto the Premiership scene.

Left foot, right foot, headers . .. it didn't matter to Robbie. They all flew in.

A treble or two from Liverpool's red-hot number nine was a pre-requisite throughout the entertaining campaigns in the mid-90s and at one point young Robbie was in serious danger of running out of places to keep his match balls.

The goals may have started to dry up in later years but it is a tribute to his exceptional talent that despite his injuries he still ranks in the top five in Liverpool's list of all-time hat-trick scorers and images of his cheeky three fingered salutes will linger long in the memory of all Kopites.

Here is how his 10 hat-tricks were scored . . .

Liverpool 5 Middlesbrough 1
December 1996

1min: Collymore picked up the ball in his own half and drove at the Boro defence before slipping the ball through to Fowler who struck a first time shot on the run under the keeper.

28mins: Slid home his 100th goal in 165 games for the club after Collymore's powerful effort had cannoned back off the near post.

77mins: Slipped McManaman's inviting pass inside the near post with the outside of his left foot.

85mins: Took Collymore's pass in his stride, shimmied his way past the last defender and coolly flicked the ball beyond the keeper.

Liverpool 3 Arsenal 1
December 1995

40mins: Collymore touched McManaman's ball into Fowler's path just outside the penalty area and although the Arsenal defence rushed to close him down, Robbie unleashed a vicious 25-yard drive into the top corner.

59mins: David James' goal-kick was flicked on by Collymore and as Fowler surged in on goal he held off the challenge of Andy Linighan to drill the ball past David Seaman.

78mins: Another treble against the Gunners was completed when his 10-yard header was fumbled into the corner by England's number one.

MOST LIVERPOOL HAT-TRICKS	
Gordon Hodgson	17
Ian Rush	16
Roger Hunt	12
Robbie Fowler	10
Michael Owen	10

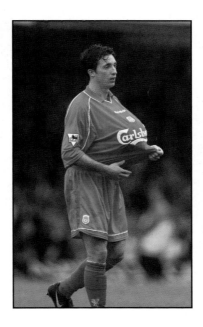

Liverpool 4 Southampton 2
October 1993

14mins: Met Rob Jones' right wing cross at the near post and flicked a downward header beyond Tim Flowers and into the far corner of the net.

29mins: Chested Neil Ruddock's cross-field ball beyond his marker before executing a sublime low finish with his right foot into the bottom corner.

85mins: The prodigious 18-year-old clinched a bizarre hat-trick when his free-kick from the right was missed by everyone, including Ian Rush, and floated directly into the far corner at the Kop end.

Three and easy: Fowler grabs the match ball after a League Cup hat-trick against Stoke

Leicester 1 Liverpool 4
October 2001

4mins: Fired home the loose ball after John Arne Riise's fierce volley from Gary McAllister's corner was only parried by Ian Walker.

43mins: Danny Murphy took advantage of a defensive error to break down the left and cut the ball back for Fowler who drilled his shot through Walker and into the net.

90mins: Smashed home his tenth hat-trick in Liverpool colours with a controlled volley into the top corner after Jari Litmanen and Vladimir Smicer had combined well down the right.

Liverpool 5 Fulham 0
October 1993

13mins: Followed up Rob Jones' 35-yard effort to net his first goal at Anfield.

20mins: Stabbed the ball home after Neil Ruddock cut the ball back across goal from an indirect free-kick.

47mins: Completed his hat-trick with a tap-in from a Rob Jones cut-back.

55mins: Met Julian Dicks' cross with a spectacular flying header.

70mins: Confidently controlled Jamie Redknapp's through-ball before despatching it with his right foot.

Stoke 0 Liverpool 8
November 2000

39mins: Gary McAllister's left wing corner was flicked on by Sami Hyypia at the near post, enabling Fowler to ghost in and bury a header past the keeper from four yards out.

82mins: Christian Ziege intercepted a Stoke City attack and played a killer ball to Robbie who raced through to strike the ball beyond the despairing dive of Carl Muggleton.

85mins: Stepped up and calmly stroked home a late spot-kick to cap a fine night's work where he scored three goals and claimed three assists.

Liverpool 5 Bolton 2
September 1995

11mins: Moved onto Jamie Redknapp's pass and after taking one touch fired his effort beyond Keith Branagan.

30mins: The Bolton defence got the offside trap all wrong allowing God to race on to David James' long kick and sweep the ball home.

46mins: A low ball in from the right from Redknapp caused chaos in the Bolton area allowing Robbie to react and stab the ball through the keeper's legs.

67mins: Collected the ball on the edge of the area and curled a stunning effort into the bottom left hand corner.

Liverpool 7 Southampton 1
January 1999

22mins: Bjornebye's corner from the left was fumbled by Saints keeper Paul Jones, allowing Fowler to prod the ball home.

37mins: Redknapp fed Michael Owen in space and he, in turn, played an incisive ball into Robbie, who dummied a first time shot before cutting inside and calmly placing the ball into the corner.

47mins: Flicked Heggem's pass wide to Owen and when the diminutive forward centred a cross, Robbie rose unmarked to loop a header beyond Jones on what was a bad day for the Saints.

Liverpool 3 Arsenal 0
August 1994

26mins: A free-kick from the right caused havoc in the Gunners' defence before breaking to Fowler who rapped the ball past David Seaman.

29mins: A mazy run from Steve McManaman took him into the penalty area and when he laid the ball to Fowler, he made no mistake, firing the ball in off the post.

31mins: John Barnes sent him through and although Seaman blocked God's first attempt he slotted his second effort in from a tight angle for the quickest hat-trick in Premiership history.

Aston Villa 2 Liverpool 4
November 1998

7mins: Stooped to power home a fantastic header after Jamie Redknapp had combined well with Michael Owen down the right wing to add to Paul Ince's second minute opener.

58mins: Collected a pass from Norwegian full-back Veggard Heggem and steadied himself before drilling a low 25-yard effort into the far corner.

66mins: Showed tremendous composure to chest down Redknapp's cross and coolly touch the ball past Michael Oakes and into the corner from eight yards out.

WARNING GOALKEEPING HAZARD

Love thy neighbours
(No matter how difficult they may make it)

IN the Anfield bible of dos and don'ts, admitting a childhood allegiance to the blue half of Merseyside isn't the most sensible of moves.

And yet when you look to some of the more iconic Reds of recent years the likes of Ian Rush, Jamie Carragher, Michael Owen and indeed Robbie Fowler are all guilty of such sacrilege.

But when you are young you can be forgiven for making mistakes and each player has since gone on to establish himself as a true Kop idol.

For Robbie, blue blood was a condition caused by family tradition.

Everton were his team and match days involved him making the journey to the other side of Stanley Park to worship the likes of Graeme Sharp and Trevor Steven.

From here he saw the error of his ways and his ability put him on the righteous path to Anfield.

By the time he had hit the goal trail with Liverpool his transformation was complete.

In his first derby appearance he scored at the Kop end, thus beginning a rollercoaster ride of ups and downs in all-Merseyside encounters.

In 17 appearances he has played the role of hero and villain on countless occasions and proved once and for all that it is with the red half of Liverpool where his heart lies.

Here are a few of the games Fowler has featured prominently in – with mixed results.

November 18, 1995
Liverpool 1 Everton 2
*one goal
A combination of heroic goalkeeping from Neville Southall and wasteful finishing condemned Liverpool to their first home defeat in a derby since 1987.

Andrei Kanchelskis' second half double did the damage and although Robbie grabbed a late lifeline on 89 minutes, it was not enough to salvage a point.

April 16, 1996
Everton 1 Liverpool 1
*one goal
At a rain-soaked Goodison Park, Fowler notched his third derby goal in five matches to snatch a share of the spoils for Roy Evans' men.

Stan Collymore's arcing cross from the left caused uncertainty

in the Everton defence, allowing Robbie to steal in and steer the ball home on the stretch.

November 20, 1996
Liverpool 1 Everton 1
*one goal
The derby goals continued to flow for Robbie when he headed Jamie Redknapp's whipped cross from the right, back across goal and into the top corner of the Everton net.

April 16, 1997
Everton 1 Liverpool 1 *sent off
A miserable derby experience for 'God.'

Not only was he sent off with eight minutes to go for a clash with David Unsworth, but he also hit the post and crossbar within a minute of each other as the Reds were held to a draw in a match they needed to win to keep their title aspirations alive.

February 23, 1998
Liverpool 1 Everton 1
Robbie's season came to a premature end in what was probably the worst moment of his career.

Having already missed a large part of pre-season and the first seven matches of the new campaign due to injury, his career was placed in serious jeopardy when he fell awkwardly following a challenge with Everton goalkeeper Thomas Myhre.

He had ruptured ligaments in his left knee, an injury that

IAN RUSH

THE master and his apprentice – Rush and Fowler.

Both were brought up as Blues, but both were destined for greatness as Reds.

With Rush in the twilight of his career and Robbie a mere rookie, the duo worked together in perfect harmony, scoring 87 goals in two seasons.

Highlights included scoring a goal apiece in the 2-1 win at home to Everton in 93/94, a Rush brace and one from Robbie in a 6-1 opening day of the season win at Crystal Palace the following season, and they were also the front two when the Reds won their only trophy under Roy Evans in the Coca-Cola Cup win over Bolton.

The signing of Stan Collymore saw Rush gradually phased out of the side, but he still enjoyed the occasional start with Robbie and they both hit doubles in a 6-0 win over Manchester City in his final season at Liverpool.

Rush's influence on his young protege was much more than just that of a team-mate, and after passing on all of his advice before leaving Liverpool, he gave the youngster his blessing to take over his crown.

"I leave with things in good hands," he said. "Robbie will probably eclipse all that I have achieved at Liverpool."

Speaking years later, in 2004, Robbie revealed that he still relied on the great man for advice and turned to him when things weren't going to plan at Manchester City.

"I spoke to Rushie quite a lot," he said. "I always listen to what he says and he still takes time out from his day to leave messages for me and that means a lot because he's an absolute legend."

This is the word of God

When Robbie has had his say

"Everything has happened really quickly for me. This is my first season and I've enjoyed every minute of it. Hopefully things can only get better."
At the end of his debut season in the first team

"It was a moral victory for us more than anything. A bit of pride was at stake and so to come back from 3-0 down to 3-3 is a great achievement – no matter who or where you are playing."
After the incredible 3-3 draw at home to Manchester United in 1994

"The Kop is brilliant to me. They are worth a goal start every game we play and when you come out the ovation you get from them is unbelievable."
Following the Kop's last stand at the end of the 1993/94 season

"It seems that the injuries I've had in my career so far have been serious ones and have led to me being out of football for months on end. I've also had some well documented problems in the past which haven't helped, but hopefully all that is behind me now. I like to think I've matured as a person over the last couple of seasons and all I want to do now is concentrate on football and playing well for Liverpool."
Talking about his injury hell, October 2000

"If you put 100 people onto a pitch you can be sure they wouldn't all find it easy to score goals. Some people find it easier than others and fortunately I've been born with the ability to find the back of the net. Obviously you can always work on your game and they say practice does make perfect, but it's much easier if you possess the natural ability from the start.
"Midfield players sometimes play in attack and they'll tell you it isn't as straightforward

as the best strikers make it look. Goalscoring is an art, and there's no better feeling than getting onto the scoresheet."
Trying to explain his natural ability to score goals, October 2000

"To get anywhere near KD (Kenny Dalglish) is an achievement which I am greatly proud of. I thought the chance had passed me by and to get the call in January asking me to come back here was fantastic. I am talking about being happy to surpass Kenny but I'm just happy about being here.
"I've kept in touch with Kenny all through my career wherever I've been, along with a few other Liverpool strikers of the past."
Describing his pride at edging past 'King' Kenny Dalglish in the all-time goalscoring charts after netting against West Brom in April, 2006. It took him up to fifth place in the list

"When I was a schoolboy at Liverpool, Kenny was manager. I met him a few times. When you are growing up you know that Kenny was a fantastic player and when he comes into the dressing room he's just got a presence about him. He used to look after the younger players."
Lauding Dalglish's influence on his career in April 2006

"Since all the injuries I don't think I'm the same player.

"It's going to be hard to get back to where I was, but I've got to keep trying and hoping.

"I've not had any setbacks as yet and I feel as good now as I have done for a while."

Admitting injuries have taken their toll in August 2004

"I want to be at Liverpool for as long as I can and if that means performing as well as I did towards the end of last season to get a new contract then so be it.

"I'm happy being back at Liverpool and if the manager plays me, he plays me. If he doesn't play me, I'll support whoever plays. But obviously it goes without saying I want to play.

"I've kept myself in good shape. I'm not going to sit here and say I'm the ultimate professional and that I've been working 24/7 in the summer. But I've done a bit and pre-season is about getting fit as well. I'm still continuing to do that so hopefully by the start of the season I'll be firing."

Assessing his situation in July 2006

"If I'm honest I've got six months to get a contract and I'm doing everything I can to get it. If it takes me being what's seen as a good boy for six months, that's what I've got to do.

"I suppose I've got to live a bit like a monk for a while. I want to stay here for a few years, and to achieve that, certain sacrifices have to be made.

"In the past people have had the wrong perception of me. There were times I did stupid things, but it was never what people made out and I'd like to think all that is behind me now."

Hoping to earn a new contract at Liverpool

"I haven't had a chance to speak to Jim's family yet but I'll speak to his wife Jean very soon.

"I know my coming back to Liverpool was what Jim would have wanted because it was he who first spotted me and brought me to the club.

"Fingers crossed I'll do well and I can make Jean and the rest of Jim's family proud of what I'm doing."

A tribute to Jim Aspinall, the former Academy youth recruitment officer who died in 2004

"After the Fulham game, I went round the chippy with my mates and got a big kiss from my mum when I got home!"

Explaining the aftermath of his five-goal demolition of Fulham in 1993

"You do stupid things when you are young and growing up but everyone has to grow out of that. I'm 25 now. I'm not a kid any more. I've got another three years left on my contract. I'm more than happy at Liverpool and my family is happy here."

On his growing maturity in May 2000

"I hate talking about football. I just do it, you know?"

The Fowler philosophy

"Anyone who doesn't learn from Ian Rush needs shooting."

On the merits of his mentor

"My phone was unbelievable. I must have had 200 text messages and about 100 calls and about 100 voicemail messages. Every one of them was fantastic and they were all saying welcome back. My little ears were burning on Friday, Saturday and Sunday.

"When I signed on Friday, Steven Gerrard and Jamie Carragher were both texting me and phoning me to find out if everything had gone smoothly. I am pleased that they were pleased as well."

Delight at the reaction to his welcome home, January 2006

"If I got a chance to put a Liverpool shirt on it could be 5002, as long as it's got the badge on the front, I don't care."

Showing he really is happy to be home, January 2006

"It happened very, very quickly for me. I don't think I played that many reserve

'After the Fulham game I got a big kiss from my mum'

games actually. At the time Liverpool were going through a transitional period.

"The game against Fulham, I couldn't believe I was on the same pitch as the likes of Ian Rush. It was just unbelievable to be on the same coach as them, never mind the same pitch. Those players were very instrumental in me settling down from a very early age.

"A lot was made about the team not doing as well but they were obviously putting chances on plates for me. I was just fortunate to be in the place where I could stick them away. The calibre of players helped me immensely."

Reflecting upon his rapid emergence in August 2004

"If you attempted to open your mouth they wouldn't knock you down a step or two, they would knock you down the full flight. I

"When I finish playing I'll always go and watch them because Liverpool are and will always be a big part of my life."
Proving he is now red through and through

"In four and a half years I scored 115 goals for him . . . and I was injured for six months or so of that. So don't give me the Spice Boy b****cks – I scored 30 goals every year for Roy Evans, and only Rushie and Roger Hunt have ever done that for Liverpool."
An autobiography rant

"I'd be a liar if I didn't say that at times I haven't played well because occasionally I've been rubbish. I'm the first to admit that."
Displaying his honesty in February 1995

"I'm not as quick as I used to be but then I wouldn't say I was ever blessed with any real pace anyway."
Displaying his honesty again in March 2006

"Regardless of what happens now I'm happy to have come back. If I do get another contract, then to use an old football cliché, I'll be over the moon."
Assessing his situation in March 2006 – before he did get a new contract

"Last season I counted four fingers at them for the number of European Cups Liverpool had won. Next time I'll stick my whole hand up."
On his hate-hate relationship with Manchester United fans

"If I'm honest, until I got married, I was always at me mum's, even when I had my own flat, and she carried on cooking and washing and ironing for me."
An insight into Robbie off the field

"Nothing had changed, except that when I went down the chippy and got me special fried rice, it would be wrapped in a newspaper that had my picture all over it."
How fame didn't change him

"Any goal for my country is nice and it is important for me to start scoring a few more for England."
An international assessment in 2001

"Ever since I started at Liverpool as a kid the fans have taken to me and any player will tell you when the supporters of your club are behind you then that helps an awful lot. I just can't thank them enough. They've given me so much support over the years and I'm grateful for that. Now I can't wait to score more goals for them and the club over the next year."
Thanks the fans for their loyalty on his return in 2006

"You go into some games knowing that you'll score goals, knowing that everything is right and your head is spot on.
"That's the feeling a striker needs, and I seemed to get it every week in the early days."
The joy of scoring

remember travelling on the bus from Anfield to Melwood when I was still at school and the amount of stick I took from the likes of Steve McMahon and Ronnie Whelan was frightening. It wasn't bad stick but it opened my eyes."
Describing how life at Anfield helped keep his feet on the ground

"I think a few of the players gave it to me because everything I touched seemed to benefit me or the team. It's a great nickname but can I just say that I never ever called myself it. It was other people but it was a great nickname and one that I am proud of."
Explaining why he has the complimentary nickname 'God'

"It was great to be back in the Ataturk Stadium as a Liverpool player. The last time I was there was as a fan, and I'd never have thought then I'd be wearing the shirt out there again 18 months later.

"To play for the club again in any stadium is a brilliant feeling, but to do it there was a bit special."
Revealing his joy after hitting a double against Galatasaray in the Ataturk

"I think a lot of that was uncalled for. The team spirit we had was very, very good. That was probably why we were the team we were; scoring lots of goals. Because we mixed off the pitch, it enabled us to be a good side on the pitch."
Responding to the Spice Boys tag

'When I finish playing I'll always go and watch them because Liverpool will always be a big part of my life'

The fans did rejoice

His followers have their say

THE words 'legend' and 'great' are so often thrown around these days that it's unfair to say Robbie is either of them. He is much greater than a great, and more legendary than your normal legend. He is God.

Like Ronnie O'Sullivan is the most natural snooker player the world has seen, Robbie is arguably the most natural goalscorer England has ever seen. Without Robbie the 1990s would not only have been unsuccessful, but also very dull.

It's a huge shame he never won a league title and didn't grace the international scene more often, but his record of almost 200 goals in less than 400 matches speaks for itself and will forever leave a mark in the history of Liverpool Football Club.

Matt Ladson, Editor, ThisIsAnfield.com.

SO many memories . . .

I will remember Robbie (aka God) for so many things; his character on and off the field, his determination to keep coming back from injury and, most importantly, for his goalscoring ability.

Robbie has always been an inspired goalscorer and you can't teach sheer natural ability.

His best moments were the League Cup final against Birmingham and his amazing volley, the UEFA Cup final the same year, his quick-fire hat-trick against Arsenal, and the moment it was announced he would be returning to Liverpool.

Robbie, you will always be a Kop legend and your feats for this club will never be forgotten.

Good luck for the future.

Andrew Grenfell, Colchester.

ROBBIE will always be remembered as a legend.

My best memories of him were his famously quick hat-trick against Arsenal and when he celebrated in the derby by snorting the line.

Geoff Ling, Liverpool.

ROBBIE Fowler's goal record is fantastic.

His stats are not quite as good as Ian Rush's, but then, he didn't have the team that Rush did, and he didn't play alongside the 'King'.

Alan Gibson, Liverpool.

HIS goals, his character, his exchange with Le Saux, his line snorting escapades, his hat-tricks – and more hat-tricks. There are so many great memories to choose from in Robbie Fowler's career.

I remember when he scored his five against Fulham - I immediately fell in love.

He also scored a brilliant goal against Aston Villa, when he received the ball in the Villa half with his back to goal and practically wearing Steve Staunton on his back. He flicked the ball between his legs with the inside of his left foot, and in the same motion, turned around

a totally bemused Staunton and lashed a vicious shot beyond the keeper. It was one of many beauties God scored for us.

A real legend, he will be sorely missed . . . again.

Tony Keown, Boston.

THERE may be more than one god, depending on what you believe, but in football there is only one Robbie Fowler.

Mike Harris, Los Angeles.

ROBBIE Fowler is a true footballing god who scored some awesome goals for us, but my personal favourite is against Alaves in the UEFA Cup final.

When he came back last winter I could not sleep for days – my heart jumped.

My best memory of him as a Liverpool player was against

'There may be more than one god, but there is only one Robbie Fowler'

Birmingham last season. He came on for Crouch and when the tannoy announcer said "number 11 Robbieeee Fowleeeer" it was amazing. What an ovation. I had tears in my eyes.

What can you say about Robbie? Just a big, huge thankyou for all your work and goals.

Steve Watkins, Crosby.

MY personal favourite memory of Robbie Fowler was a match at Arsenal.

Robbie had a one-on-one with David Seaman and when the Arsenal keeper collected the ball, Fowler jumped over him. The referee immediately awarded a penalty.

David Seaman couldn't believe it. The Arsenal team couldn't believe it. And nor could Robbie.

He picked himself up and started waving his hands, gesturing to the referee as if to say, 'no ref, it wasn't a foul'. Robbie even apologised to Seaman before stepping up to take the spot-kick.

It just shows the sportsmanship of the guy and that Robbie is a true gentleman. How many players in the diving culture of today would do the same thing?

And for that, I will always remember Robbie as a true Liverpool legend and he will be sorely missed.

Oh, and not to forget the five goals he scored against Fulham!

Simon Pearce, Darlington.

SADLY for Robbie, especially in the early days of his career, he was a diamond surrounded by pieces of glass – though it's taken me many years of watching and appreciating football to realise it.

Having grown up watching Rush, Souness and co, I don't think I appreciated Robbie Fowler as I should have done, especially when he played in a side which used to frustrate me so much.

When we sold him to Leeds I must admit I was actually pleased, but over the years I realise he was a true Red, especially when he used to give the four or five-finger salute to the Stretford End!

Robbie deserves every accolade and testimony he gets because he is one of those players about who you can say to your kids and grandkids 'I saw Robbie Fowler play'.

Bob Jones, Liverpool.

OF all his outstanding goals, the quick hat-trick in the 94/95 season will always stand out – pure class.

There's no shame in Robbie

leaving now. It's like some part of him has been put to rest, having been back for the last 18 months. He's proven that he is still among the best strikers still playing.

Andy Davies, Johannesburg.

BESIDES the quick hat-trick against Arsenal and snorting the line, I also remember how happy I was to see his goal in Dortmund. I wanted to see him play in that final so much and when he was on, I also wanted to see him score. When he did I was so happy.

Liam Pulford, Chester.

ROBBIE Fowler is a true goalscoring genius – the most natural finisher this club has ever had. I was over the moon when Rafa brought him back.

Also, thanks to Stuart Pearce for not standing in Robbie's way when Liverpool came knocking.

Robbie is God and always will be.

Kev Marshall, Haydock.

ROBBIE Fowler has given me more happiness than any other Liverpool player. His style of play is what I tried to copy, and his name was the one I used to call out when playing in the park.

Unlike a player like Michael Owen, there was always a feeling with Robbie that he was one of us.

He is a player who deserved more and should have achieved more.

Alec Gilbody, Edinburgh.

I USED to go to a few games a year when I was a kid but I got my season ticket in time for the 1993/94 season – the year Robbie Fowler came into the side.

I don't know what we would have done without him and Steve McManaman at that time.

Anyway, Robbie turned up and brought pace and excitement to a slow and mediocre team. I'd take the partnership of Robbie and Rushie in the mid 1990s over any other partnership we've had since.

Mark Tyrrell, Liverpool.

Need a pick-me-up this summer?

Then pick up your copy of LFC magazine – the ideal tonic for the cricket season

Out every Tuesday – 52 weeks of the year (Subscriptions hotline on 0845 143 0001)

The word of his disciples

What the professionals think of Robbie

"THERE aren't many strikers around like Robbie any more, not just in England but in Europe.

"In his prime he was one of the best finishers there's ever been. When you think he took the number nine shirt from Ian Rush and managed to fill it, I don't think there's a bigger tribute you can pay to him than that.

"The number nine shirt at Anfield is one of the most important and it's been great to see Robbie wearing it again."
STEVEN GERRARD in May 2007

"ROBBIE reminds me a lot of Jimmy Greaves in that he has a similar kind of coolness and doesn't have to blast them in. He is such a natural. He knows where the goal is and what position to take up. You can't teach anybody that.

"But what I really like about him is that he takes his chances so early. He doesn't have to stop the ball. He just helps it on."
ROGER HUNT in 1995

"I THINK Robbie has shown us yet again that he's a legend.

"It's hard when you're not in the squad all the time, and not always playing, and yet he scored twice and also played really well.

"He's very important for the team, even when he's not on the pitch with us. It's unbelievable the way he finishes his penalties. He's still got a very cool head and is a very good player."
DIRK KUYT pays tribute to the 'legend' Robbie Fowler, February 2007

"AS a finisher, he is an absolute killer inside the penalty area. What sets him apart is the way he takes advantage of half chances when the ball is loose. He is lethal when that happens.

"Robbie has created an excellent atmosphere in the dressing room. He's a very opinionated man and he's very, very funny. Robbie definitely represents the great sense of humour that Liverpudlians are famous for!"
XABI ALONSO praises God's abilities both on and off the field, April 2006

"FOR me it's an honour just to be in the same team as him because he's been such a great player over the years, and obviously with myself being a striker you watch players like him and learn from him."
PETER CROUCH admits he is honoured to play alongside Robbie, April 2006

"I WON'T be ringing him. He's now scored more goals than me so I'm not talking to him. In fact, I wish he hadn't come back. Whose bright idea was that?"
The wry wit of King KENNY DALGLISH, April 2006

"I SPENT my younger years being very aware of football and watching it all the time on the television, but even if you don't watch the game then I'm sure you'd still know who Robbie Fowler is.

"He's a real idol to the fans here and I think he's partly responsible for people going to the game almost with an extra spring in their step

because they know they can expect something special from him."
FERNANDO MORIENTES speaks glowingly about Fowler 'the idol', April 2006

"EVERYONE raved about Robbie and many Liverpool fans say he's on a par with the best they've seen. He used to love training, he played with a smile on his face and he adored the feeling that came with scoring goals.

"He was a joy to play with and he still gets an incredible reception at Anfield. But leaving the club was the worst thing he did. Gerard Houllier was right to sell him and no-one would've said it was a backwards step going to Leeds.

"But if you'd have said to me five or six years ago 'where do you expect Fowler to be in five or six years' time?' I would've said Real Madrid, not City, with all due respect to them."
JAN MOLBY is saddened by the demise of Fowler, September 2004

"HE often shoots early, he doesn't mind where he shoots from, but he seems to get late fade on his shots like a golfer. He usually gets ten out of ten shots on target, and with nine

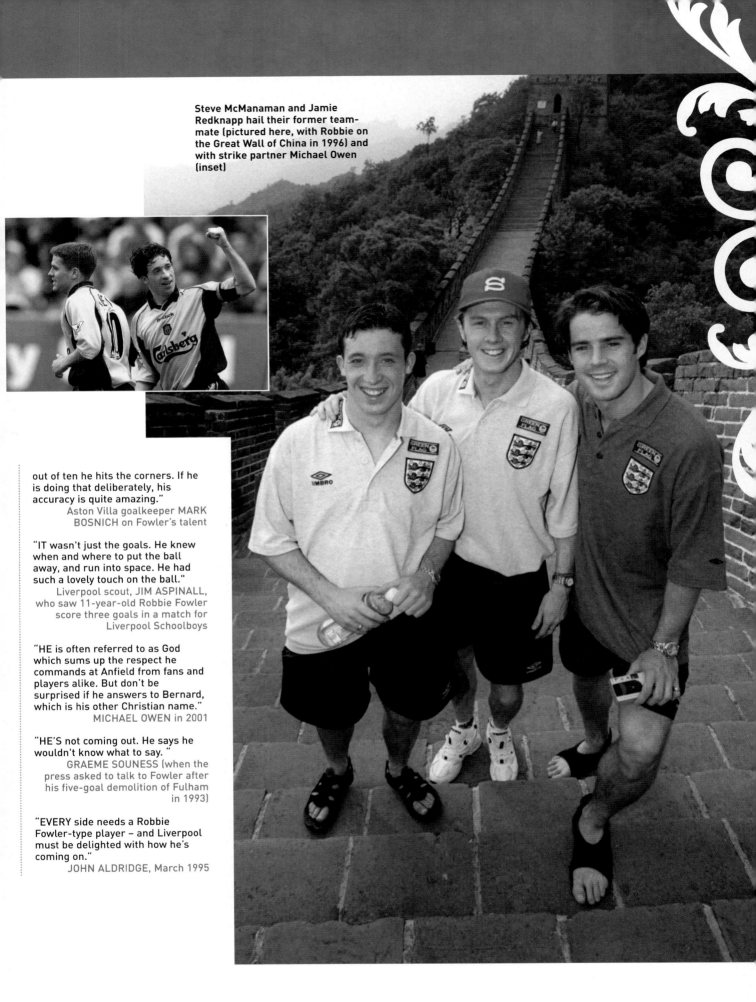

Steve McManaman and Jamie Redknapp hail their former team-mate (pictured here, with Robbie on the Great Wall of China in 1996) and with strike partner Michael Owen (inset)

out of ten he hits the corners. If he is doing that deliberately, his accuracy is quite amazing."
   Aston Villa goalkeeper MARK BOSNICH on Fowler's talent

"IT wasn't just the goals. He knew when and where to put the ball away, and run into space. He had such a lovely touch on the ball."
   Liverpool scout, JIM ASPINALL, who saw 11-year-old Robbie Fowler score three goals in a match for Liverpool Schoolboys

"HE is often referred to as God which sums up the respect he commands at Anfield from fans and players alike. But don't be surprised if he answers to Bernard, which is his other Christian name."
   MICHAEL OWEN in 2001

"HE'S not coming out. He says he wouldn't know what to say. "
   GRAEME SOUNESS (when the press asked to talk to Fowler after his five-goal demolition of Fulham in 1993)

"EVERY side needs a Robbie Fowler-type player – and Liverpool must be delighted with how he's coming on."
   JOHN ALDRIDGE, March 1995

"HE'S such a talent and he was an absolute model in training in Austria. He's a terrific prospect."
KEVIN KEEGAN, March 1995 – as part of the England U21 set up

"I WAS thrilled for Robbie. He deserves everything he gets.
"It was a bit of a shame that he was put on his own up front against three big centre-halves. But I hope he goes on to become England centre forward for the next 10-15 years."
STEVE McMANAMAN praises Robbie after he made his England debut, March 1996

"YOU can see in training that Robbie is a goal machine. Everybody knows that he needs to work on his fitness at the moment but we know that he can score goals."
JOHN ARNE RIISE, February 2006

"FOWLER was excellent. I thought the partnership between him and Michael Owen up front was excellent."
SVEN GORAN ERIKSSON on Fowler's 'excellent' display in a friendly against Mexico in 2001

"ROBBIE'S got everything for me. He's a fantastic goalscorer at such a young age and bangs in goals for fun. I've never seen anyone so good at his age. I'm just so pleased he plays for Liverpool."
JAMIE REDKNAPP, 1996 on 21-year-old Robbie

"I THINK Robbie Fowler, for his age and what's he doing, is proving he is good enough to play for England. He's scoring goals left, right and centre and for his age he is magnificent."
JASON McATEER, 1996

"ROBBIE Fowler's had an outstanding season, not just at Liverpool Football Club, but in the country. He's up there along with Cantona, Gullit and Ferdinand."
JOHN SCALES, 1996

"I THINK we have to be happy Fowler is being overlooked. He would probably be the most dangerous player for England this summer."
Current Scotland boss ALEX McLEISH is fearful of Fowler's prowess leading up to the England v Scotland clash in April 1996

"WE call him God because he does wonderful things."
JASON McATEER, 1997

"A MARVELLOUS talent with magnificent goalscoring ability . . . and little ears."
STEVE McMANAMAN on his pal Robbie in 1997

HOW TO MAKE SURE YOU'RE WELL RED

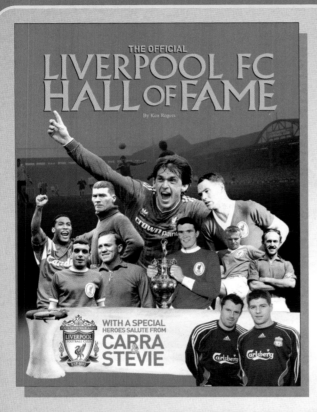

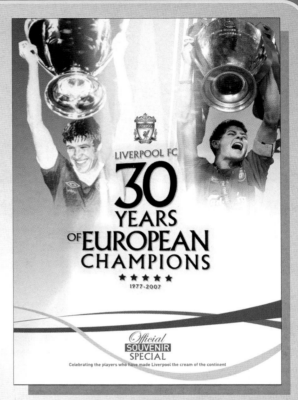

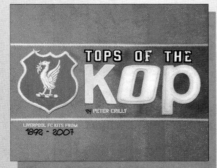

Official Liverpool FC Hall of Fame book
£20 per copy
plus free p&p (UK only)
The men voted the club's greatest legends with introduction by Carra and Stevie

30 Years of European Champions
£3.99 plus p&p
Celebrate the 40 players to have won a European Cup winners medal with Liverpool

Tops of the Kop
£8.99 plus free p&p
A fascinating look at the changing face of Liverpool's kit down the years. This book showcases kits from 1892 to the present adidas era

'WE'VE WON IT 5 TIMES'

To celebrate Liverpool's five European Cup wins from 1977 to 2005 you can buy any 5 prints from our exclusive collection for just £25
(plus £1.50 p&p).
Usual price £50 - a saving of £25!

Go to **WWW.MERSEYSHOP.COM/PHOTOS** to make your selection and look at other great photos & gift ideas or call **0151 472 2549** to place your order.

WWW.MERSEYSHOP.COM   0845 143 0001

FOWLER!

Fowler 26: 80-81

Stats entertainment

Where Robbie stands in the Liverpool goal tables

Another penalty hits the back of the net, adding to Robbie's formidable record from 12 yards

PENALTY SUCCESSES

1 Jan Molby 42
2 Phil Neal 38
3 Billy Liddell 35
4 Tommy Smith 22
5 Robbie Fowler 20 out of 26
6 John Aldridge 17
7 Terry McDermott 16
8 Gordon Hodgson 15
9 Michael Owen 13
10 Kevin Keegan 11

PENALTY MISSES

1 Phil Neal 11
2 Michael Owen 10
3 Tommy Smith 9
4 Robbie Fowler 6
5 Billy Liddell 6
6 Kevin Keegan 6
7 John Barnes 5
8 Ronnie Moran 5
9 Steven Gerrard 4
10 Terry McDermott 4

LEAGUE CUP GOALS

1 Ian Rush 48
2 Robbie Fowler 29
3 Kenny Dalglish 27
4 Ronnie Whelan 14
5 Steve McMahon 13
6 Danny Murphy 11
7 David Fairclough 10
8 Steve McManaman 10
9 David Johnson 9
10 Jan Molby 9

GOALS IN ALL COMPETITIONS

1 Ian Rush 346
2 Roger Hunt 286
3 Gordon Hodgson 241
4 Billy Liddell 228
5 Robbie Fowler 183
6 Kenny Dalglish 172
7 Michael Owen 158
8 Harry Chambers 151
9 Jack Parkinson 130
10 Sam Raybould 128

Those who have felt God's wrath

Aston Villa	14
Arsenal	12
Charlton	8
Fulham	8
Leeds United	8
Southampton	8
Chelsea	7
Newcastle	7
Tottenham	7
Bolton	6
Derby	6
Everton	6
Manchester United	6
Middlesbrough	6
Nottingham Forest	6
Leicester City	5
West Ham	5
Crystal Palace	4
Man City	4
Blackburn Rovers	3
Brann Bergen	3
Sheffield United	3
Sion	3
Stoke City	3
Wimbledon	3
Burnley	2
Galatasaray	2
Ipswich	2
Kosice	2
Norwich	2
Oldham	2
Sheff Weds	2
Sunderland	2
WBA	2
Alaves	1
Birmingham City	1
Coventry City	1
FC Haka	1
Paris St Germain	1
Port Vale	1
Portsmouth	1
QPR	1
Reading	1
Rochdale	1
Shrewsbury	1
Strasbourg	1
Tranmere	1
Wycombe	1

LIVERPOOL CAREER GOALS AND APPEARANCES

Season	Lge	FAC	LgeCup	Euro	Total	Apps
93/94	12	0	6	0	18	34
94/95	25	2	4	0	31	57
95/96	28	6	2	0	36	53
96/97	18	1	5	7	31	44
97/98	9	0	3	1	13	28
98/99	14	1	1	2	18	35
99/00	3	0	0	0	3	14
00/01	8	2	6	1	17	48
01/02	3	0	0	1	4	17
05/06	5	0	0	0	5	16
06/07	3	0	2	2	7	23
Totals	128	12	29	14	183	369

*Left in November 2001, returned in January 2006

THE FOWLER GRAPH
OF FAN POPULARITY

YOU'D SHARE
YOUR WIFE
WITH HIM

GOD-LIKE

DEMI-GOD

**STAR
STATUS**

YOU'D GO
FOR A PINT
WITH HIM

POPULAR

AVERAGE

Given FIFA Fair Play award for trying to persuade the referee to reverse his awarding of a penalty against Arsenal

Penalised by the FA for mocking Graeme Le Saux and pretending to snort a white line during a derby

Wore t-shirt in support of Liverpool dockers

Finishes season with 36 goals and makes squad for England's Euro 96 campaign

Struck down by major knee injury and misses 1998 World Cup

England debut (v Bulgaria)

PFA Young Player of the Year for the first time

First cup final win (v Bolton in the Coca Cola Cup)

Scores a five minute hat-trick against Arsenal

Debut for England U21s

First league hat-trick (v Southampton)

5 goals against Fulham

Debut goal against Fulham

1993   1994   1995   1996   1997   1998   1999